edward de bono's
mind
power

edward de bono's
mind
power

DORLING KINDERSLEY
LONDON • NEW YORK • STUTTGART • MOSCOW

A DORLING KINDERSLEY BOOK

Art editor	Mark Johnson Davies
Editor	Neil Lockley
DTP designer	Zirrinia Austin
Assistant designer	Stephen Croucher
Project editor	Louise Candlish
Managing editor	Sean Moore
Production controller	Meryl Silbert
Picture research	Lorna Ainger
DK Picture Library	Caroline Potts

First published in Great Britain in 1995
by Dorling Kindersley Limited,
9 Henrietta Street, London WC2E 8PS

Reprinted (twice) in 1996

Visit us on the World Wide Web at
http://www.dk.com

A CIP catalogue record for this book is available from the
British Library

ISBN 0 7513 0190 6

Colour reproduction by Colourscan, Singapore

Manufactured in China by Imago

contents

how to enjoy thinking

Your brain is the MOST
IMPORTANT thing you have.

*Then why don't you enjoy
using it?* Because thinking
is *hard work* and *serious*,
and even BORING.

How many hours a week do you spend watching television? Twenty? Twenty-five? Thirty? And how many hours listening to music? And how many hours actively using your brain? Watching television is very enjoyable, but passive. Listening to music may exercise your feelings, but not your brain.

Some people believe that thinking is just a matter of intelligence. They assume that if you are born with a high IQ then you can think, and if not, then it is just too bad. This is complete nonsense. In my experience, many highly intelligent people are bad thinkers. They know how to defend their point of view, but that is all. Many people with a lower IQ are much better thinkers.

Intelligence is like the horsepower of a car. A powerful car has the *potential* to drive at speed. But you can have a powerful car and drive it badly. Someone with a less powerful car may be a better driver. Like the horsepower of a car, intelligence is just a potential. Thinking is the driving skill with which each individual drives his or her intelligence.

Would you rather be a good driver or a bad driver?

Anyone can develop a high degree of skill in thinking if he or she wants to do so. That means making some effort. That is the purpose of this book: to make it easy to develop your personal skill in thinking. There is no point in expecting schools, or even universities, to develop your thinking skill for you. In my experience, very few do. Even where thinking is taught, this is usually of the analytical and critical type. This is useful, but it is only one part of thinking.

So it is up to you.

Thinking is not a matter of getting the right answer. It is a matter of consciously using your mind, and enjoying using it. Treat thinking like a sport. Have fun. In sport, training may be boring at times, but you know you are getting better all the time as you train.

Why bother to learn thinking? Why not just pick it up as you go along? Because *the sort of thinking you will just pick up may be very limited*. In any sport, coaching makes a big difference. IT IS THE SAME WITH THINKING.

This book covers some of the basic aspects of thinking. There is "perception". How do we choose to look at the world? There is the "power of possibilities". This is what has been behind the success of Western civilization in science and technology. There is the generation of "alternatives" that give us more freedom of action. There is "choice and decision", because we may sometimes have to choose between alternatives. "Judgement" is important, and so is "analysis". Then there are "values and feelings". All these things, and more, are part of the skill of thinking.

In this book you can read a little bit about these aspects of thinking. But, more importantly, you can get to practise each aspect of thinking with exercises and games that have been devised specially for this book. They have also been designed to be fun and enjoyable, and to be repeated again and again.

You should not feel that you always have to get things right, or always have to win at the games. You try, and you enjoy trying, and by trying you improve. You do not give up tennis because every first serve does not work. In time, more and more of your first serves will succeed.

It is the fun of thinking that matters most – not the result. Watch yourself thinking.

For the young, as you become a more and more skilled thinker you will find that this has a powerful effect on your school work and examinations. In later life, skilled thinking will be of use in both personal matters and work matters. A thinker can take initiatives instead of waiting to be told what to do. A thinker can generate useful alternatives and make decisions. A thinker can solve problems and design ways forward.

Go through the book slowly and carefully, and try out the exercises. Knowing and doing are two different things. You can know all about a sport such as tennis, but you will only become a tennis player when you begin to practise playing the game.

The *exercises* in this book will help you to put your thinking skills into practice. Some of the exercises can be done on your own, but many are more fun if done with a friend, or with a group. The *games* require another player. It could be someone in your family, or a friend. Make it a joint venture with a friend to develop your thinking skills together. Adapt the rules of the games to suit your need. Don't just play the games once. Repeat them and repeat them and watch your thinking skills improve.

Make THINKING your HOBBY

Edward de Bono

WHAT IS IT?

recognition

You get through life by

dealing with the things you know.

It would be useful if everything

were LABELLED.

APPLE

SHIP

FLY

KETTLE

In fact, most things *are* labelled, but the labels are supplied in our minds. You write your own labels. Once the label is in place, you know what to do with that thing. You *eat* an ice-cream. You use a bus *to travel.*

When you take an apple out of a box labelled "apples", then you expect that apple to *taste* just as apples should taste. Once the label is clearly fixed to the box, then you know immediately what you are getting out of the box. You do not need to recognize the thing all over again. You just trust the label on the box. You could sit in the dark and eat apples out of a box labelled "apples" without any surprises.

Just as our minds put LABELS on all the things with which we are familiar, so our minds put all the things with the *same label into the same box.*

This is a very powerful system. When we recognize something, we put it into a familiar labelled box. Then we remember the "instructions" on that box and we know what we should do with that thing. We have either written the instructions ourselves, or we have borrowed them from someone else. All of this helps to make life extremely tidy and convenient, and very much easier.

The easy part is getting something out of a labelled box. The more difficult part is knowing which box to put something into. Does it go here or does it go there? You come across what looks like a mushroom. Is it something that is good to eat, or is it poisonous?

A

C

It is possible that we might be able to make a guess at what something is. However, if the item in question is completely unfamiliar to us, then we can only wait until we can borrow the label and the instructions from someone else.

B

D

CAN YOU GUESS WHICH of the four types of mushrooms shown here are edible and which are poisonous? Check your answers on pages 70-71 ☞

WHAT IS IT?
30 QUESTIONS

One player shuffles the cards, then looks at the top card. No-one else can see this card. The other player(s) must then discover what the card shows by asking up to 30 questions. Any question that requires only a "yes" ▶

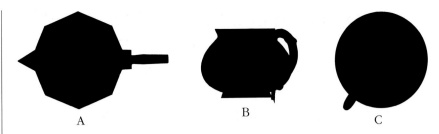

A   B   C

HOW QUICKLY can you identify these three items simply by glancing at their silhouettes? Check your answers on pages 70-71 ☞

There are times when something is very familiar but we cannot get a full look at it. So we have to carry out the recognition from parts of the whole picture. We call these parts

CLUES

▶ *or "no" answer counts as one question. A question that requires a fuller answer (for example, "Where is this used?") counts as five questions. A guess question counts as three questions.*

If the object remains undiscovered, the player answering the questions wins. Otherwise, the person making the winning guess is the winner. The game continues with another player taking over and drawing a card.

A

B

C

D

THESE PICTURES show sections of some very familiar faces. Can you recognize the faces? Check your answers on pages 70-71 ☞

40 QUESTIONS: THE MIXED UP THINKARD GAME

This game is very similar to the "30 Questions" game (see page 15). The procedure and scoring are exactly the same, but this time the game is very much harder. Two cards ▶

THESE IMAGES ARE broken-up pieces of a painting. What do you think

is happening? For the complete picture, see pages 70-71 ☞

▶ are drawn, and the person holding the cards has to answer for both cards, but without saying which is which.

The answers might go as follows: "Yes, for one of them"; "No, for both of them"; "One of them can be used in the..."

The questions have to sort out one or both of the items. Because this game is more difficult than the "30 Questions" game, 40 questions are allowed.

Sometimes, the clues are all present but they are not together and they are all mixed-up. This makes it much more difficult to recognize something.

Sometimes, we cannot actually see the object but are only told about it. We have to put the verbal clues together. Often, clues are not given and we have to ask for them. This might be what a detective does. A scientist also has to ask for clues by doing experiments.

Sometimes, when we cannot get as full a look as we would like, it is difficult to recognize things that we know well. But if we are not certain about something, or do not know it, then the fullest of looks may be no good.

COMMENT

You will find as you play the "30" and "40 Questions" games that you learn to devise questions that draw out the relevant clues.

This system of recognizing something and then putting it into a box in our minds has a lot of advantages. It makes life simpler. All you have to do is to recognize something, and then you know what to do about it.

But there are also a lot of dangers that can arise from this system. The boxes may be very simple and crude, and so we are forced to see the world in this crude and simple way. For instance, if you just had two boxes labelled

then you would have to put everyone you knew into one of these two boxes. So you would be treating as friends people who were not really your friends. And you would be treating as enemies people who were not your enemies at all.

Another danger of this system is that boxes are always based on the past. They are, therefore, not very good at dealing with the future. For example, early computers were extremely complicated to use. So someone who had only used early computers might well feel that all computers were complicated to use.

On certain occasions, we may also create labelled boxes out of only very limited experience. For instance, if a red-haired person bullied you at school, you might think that all red-haired people were bullies. The more boxes that you manage to develop, the more effective and useful your actions will be.

A

B

CAN YOU IDENTIFY the eight flags shown here?

C

D

COMMENT

Unless you already have the labels, you will find it difficult to put a name to the flags.

E

F

Check your answers on pages 70-71

G

H

COMMENT

Once you have checked the answers, you will have "borrowed" labels.

concepts

Our minds are experienced in

RECOGNIZING and LINKING two items

that are *"similar"*.

TYPEWRITER   CAKE   CAR   HEN

HORSE   PENCIL   SNAKE   PAINT

CAN YOU ARRANGE the eight items shown above into four pairs? Each pair must share a concept. Check possible answers on pages 70-71 ☞

COMMENT

There are no "right" answers to the concept exercise above. The answers on pages 70-71 are just a few possible sets of pairs. Yours may be different, but will be just as "right".

As soon as we are asked to put items into pairs, we look for something that two items have in common. In the above exercise, a typewriter is very different from a pencil and would never go into a box labelled "pencils". Yet both pencils and typewriters are writing devices. This is a "concept" that links them together. We might have a group of items that includes chalk, pencil, typewriter, computer, felt-tip pen, ball-point pen, and fountain pen.

COMMENT

When you have made your pairings, try and make four new ones. Then try and find a concept that links each of the four items in the top row with the item beneath it.

Objects that appear quite *different* at first can often be *connected* by a COMMON CONCEPT.

STUDY CAREFULLY THE ITEMS featured below. As you can see, there are eight distinct and separate items. Can you divide the featured items into two clearly differentiated groups, each numbering four items? Use any basis that you like to create the two groups. Pause and do your own thinking before you read on.

BOAT   TREE   ANT   DUCK

PIG   TAP   CLOCK   CLOUD

In the above grouping exercise, you might have decided that boat, tree, and clock can be grouped together on the basis that they all have (or can have) some wood in them. You might have decided that the duck, the pig, and the ant are all animals and the others are not. But that is only three items. Thinking further, you might decide that duck, cloud, boat, and tap are all connected with water.

These are just some of the possible groupings that you might have thought of. You might have decided on your grouping on a totally different basis.

COMMENT

Once you have made your groupings, try and find *another* concept that links each group of four. Later, try and find concepts that link five, six, seven, or all eight items.

THINKARD
GAME

**CONCEPT
SNAP**

---

*This game is for two
players. The pack is
divided into two and
each player is dealt
half of the pack. This
is facing downwards.*

---

*Each player now turns
over their top card at
exactly the same
moment. This must
be done by turning
the card outwards
(if the card were
turned inwards, the
person turning it
would see it before the
other player). When
the cards are visible,
a player says "snap"* ▶

It can be easy to group items

on the basis of a *broad concept.*

It is more difficult to recognize the

NARROWER CONCEPTS involved.

THESE FOUR TYPES OF ships are linked by the broad concept that they each move forward through water. What are the narrower concepts involved? Pause and do your own thinking before reading on.

SAILING SHIP   PADDLE STEAMER

SCREW SHIP   HOVERCRAFT

In the above exercise, there is a similarity between the screw ship and the paddle steamer. In both cases, there is some surface pushing against the water. In both cases, the energy is provided by an engine, in one case driving a screw-propeller and, in the other, driving a paddle-wheel.

The hovercraft and sailing ship both get their motion through operating in the air. The sailing ship uses the energy of the wind. The hovercraft uses a propeller to push itself forward. In a way, the concept of the sailing ship is different from all the others, because it requires no added input of energy, but relies on the natural energy of the wind.

*▶ if he or she can see a
"concept connection"
between the cards. The
players can agree to
exclude some simple
connections, such
as "both contain
some metal".*

---

*The same concept
connection should not
be made more than
once in each game.
The player who says
"snap" first and then
follows it up with
an explanation of
the concept
connection takes all
the cards from the
other player that have
been turned over
up to that point. The
game continues until
one player has no
cards left or until
an agreed time
has been reached.
The player with
the most cards
wins the game.*

BROADER CONCEPTS

One player picks a card at random from the pack and places it face upwards on the table. Each player in turn has to suggest a concept that includes the item on the card.

The concept must be related in some way to the function of the item. Each new concept can be broader or narrower than the previous one. But if the new concept makes too big a jump, then the next player can suggest a concept that is in-between the new concept and the previous one. ▶

ZEPPELIN

PLANE

HELICOPTER

HOT AIR BALLOON

ROCKET

ALL THESE THINGS CAN move through the air. Some of the similarities are easy to recognize. For example, the zeppelin and hot air balloon are both lighter than air, and the plane and the helicopter both fly using wings. But what are the different concepts involved? And why is the rocket different from the other four?

Check for suggestions on pages 70-71 ☞

A son has a father but the father
is the son of someone else.
And that father is *also* a son.
In the same way, a CONCEPT
may define a GROUP but may
also be part of a second and
LARGER GROUP – and so on.

▶ For example, if the item on the card is a bucket, player "A" might suggest: "A way of transporting water." Player "B" might suggest a narrower concept: "A portable container for water." A concept in between the two might be: "Getting water to where you need it." Once every player has suggested a concept, the game continues with a new card.

COMMENT

A variant of this game is as follows: turn over a card, agree a concept; turn over another card and find a concept that links the two; and so on. You will improve each time you play.

WHAT COULD IT BE?

possibilities

We like to be certain. We like to be sure. We want to know that what we are eating is definitely an edible mushroom and not, in fact, a poisonous toadstool.

Yet possibilities are the

DRIVING FORCE of human thinking

and human *progress*.

A   B   C

WHAT ARE THE OBJECTS shown in this distorted way?
Check your answers on pages 70-71 ☞

Possibilities allow us to deal with new or old things that we
cannot see clearly.
We may put forward a possibility in our minds and then
work to check that possibility out.

A

B

C

D

E

THINKARD
GAME
**THE
DISCOVERY
GAME**

———

*The cards are laid face
upwards on the table.
One player chooses
a card because the
object shown on the
card contains a
particular feature
(for example: "It has
wheels"; "It needs
electricity"). The other
player has to carry out
"experiments" in order
to find the hidden
feature. This player is
the "experimenter".*

———

*The experimenter
chooses a card which
be or she thinks may
contain the hidden
feature. This is put
forward as an
"experiment". The* ▶

OF THE FIVE SHAPES SHOWN above, one is the "odd man out".
Which one could it be and why? Check your answers on pages 70-71 ☞

Possibilities and guessing go hand-in-hand. We naturally prefer to work from certainty rather than from a guess. But the guess gives us something to work on, so that we can eventually arrive at certainty.

In the above exercise, we need to work out which shape has been chosen as the "odd man out". We start by making a guess. Then we check out this guess against the other shapes. If it turns out that none of the other shapes possess the "guessed" feature, then we can say that this is at least one of the bases on which the shape has been chosen.

Science works in exactly the same way. There is evidence, data, or information. Then someone makes a guess as to what is going on. In science, this type of possibility is called an "hypothesis". We can then look at the evidence through this hypothesis to see if things fit. We can look for further evidence to check out the hypothesis. We can design experiments to check out the hypothesis.

Sometimes, we cannot move from possibility to certainty. The best we can do is move from possibility to probability.

▶ *first player says "yes"
or "no", depending
on whether the
experiment card
contains the bidden
feature. The successful
cards are placed on
the same level as the
original card.*

———

*The unsuccessful cards
are placed a level
below. When the
experimenter thinks
that he or she has the
answer, this is
put forward.*

———

*This game can be
made very difficult if
the first player chooses
two features instead
of just one. For
example: "It needs
electricity to work and
can be useful in the
garden". This more
difficult version of
the game should
only be used after
much experience with
the simpler version
in which there
is only one
bidden feature.*

In technology, there is a "vision" of a possibility. Then we set out to find ways of making that possibility happen. The tunnel under the Channel separating England from France was somebody's vision. Then ways of making it happen had to be worked out in detail.

THE PICTURE SHOWS a box standing on its edge on a table.
There is no fixed support. Why is the box standing on its corner?
Can you make a box do the same thing?
You are not allowed to fix the box to the table in any way.
Check your answers on pages 70-71 Check your answers on pages 70-71 ☞

In the above exercise, there are two things that you may want to know. The first thing is how this particular box has been made to stand on its edge. The second thing is how any box can be made to stand on its edge. In the second case, you may be able to design other ways of doing it that are totally different from the one that has actually been used. The first case is like science. You set out to discover what is actually happening. The second case is more like technology. You create new possibilities.

NUMBER
CARD GAME
**THE
SEQUENCE
GAME**

One player chooses
a sequence of four
numbers: for example,
3 - 7 - 11 - 15. The
other person has to
produce as many
possibilities as he or
she can for the choice
of this sequence. The
relationship between
the numbers must, of
course, be consistent
and should not
change as the
sequence develops.

Note that the sequence
is all important.
It is not a matter
of putting together
numbers that just
happen to have some
feature in common.
In the example given
you simply add four
to one number to
get the next number.
In the sequence
4 - 7 - 13 - 25, you
add the number ▶

The brain can only see what it has been *prepared* to see. So unless we prepare the brain by *creating possibilities,* we are unable to see NEW PATTERNS and NEW IDEAS.

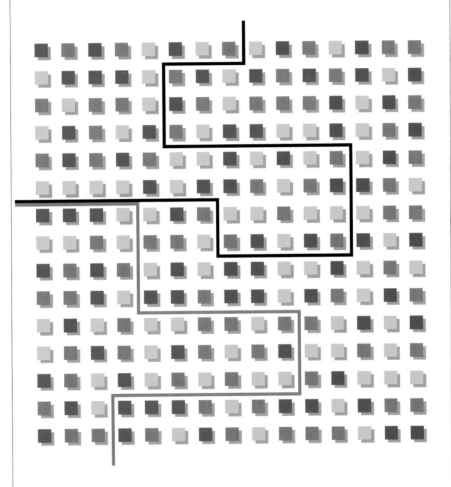

THE DIAGRAM ABOVE shows a maze. Imagine that a robot cart has been programmed to find its ways through the maze by following certain rules. The black line shows one route that the cart has taken. The red line shows the route that is taken when the rules have been changed. What are the two sets of rules? Check your answers on pages 70-71 ☞

It is only when we have discovered or created a range of possibilities that we are adequately prepared to exercise our judgement.

▶ to itself and then
subtract one. The basis
of the sequence may
be quite complex.

The Sequence Game
works differently for
each player. The
player who is trying
to find the sequence
is in the position of a
scientist who is trying
to discover the "truth"
or "possible truths".

When playing the
"Number Card" games
for the first time, use
cards 1-20. When
playing the games on
subsequent occasions,
use as many of the
cards as you wish.

COMMENT

Once you have
worked out the two
different sets of rules,
devise your own set
of rules for crossing
the maze.

judgement

In some ways, judgement is the most fundamental operation of human thinking.

does this match?
DOES THIS FIT?
is this right?

In our minds we have an idea of how things should be. We then judge whether something matches this idea. Recognition is based on judgement. You see an unusual-looking cat or dog. Does this match your mental picture of a cat or dog? Or does it challenge it? If you are the expert judge at a dog show, you choose the winning animal by seeing which dog best matches the "right" shape for each different breed.

Experience gives us mental pictures of how things work and what happens under different circumstances. We then judge whether our actions are "right" depending upon whether these actions fit our mental pictures.

DOES THIS Sphynx cat match your mental picture of a cat?

DOES THIS Neapolitan mastiff match your mental picture of a dog?

There are rules in playing any game. There are traffic rules. There are rules of law. There are rules of grammar and rules of mathematics. We judge whether something is "right" depending on whether it follows or matches those rules.

THE LINES SHOWN BELOW are of different widths and different colours. Their positions are different. Can you "judge" which of these lines are equal in length to line "A"? Do not use any measuring method. Do it by eye. Check your answers on pages 70-71 ☞

Though we often pretend otherwise, judgement of many things is not always easy. There are "maybe" situations. We may have to make a DECISION. Sometimes, the decision is not as firmly based as we would like.

THINKARD
GAME
**MEMORY
JUDGEMENT**

*Sixteen cards are laid
face upwards in
a four-by-four grid.
The players observe
the cards for 20
seconds. The cards
are then turned
face downwards.*

*Each player takes
turns predicting the
card he or she is about
to turn over. If the
prediction is correct,
the player keeps the
card. If the prediction
is wrong, the opponent
gets the card.* ▶

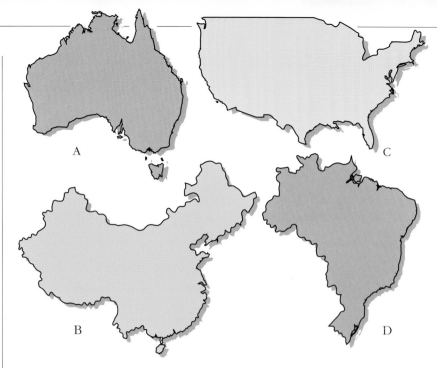

A

B

C

D

CAN YOU IDENTIFY the countries above by their shapes and sizes?
The possibilities are: Brazil, Australia, Greenland, Canada, Argentina, Russia
China, and the USA. Check your answers on pages 70-71 ☞

Every time we judge something, we are
judging it against some EXPERIENCE or
EXPECTATION or *feeling*. A scientist has
a *feeling* for his or her subject. A cook
has a *feeling* of what tastes right.

▶ *The game continues
until no cards are left.
The winner is the
player with most cards.*

*This game can also be
played in another way.
Two players each lay
out a set of 12 cards
face upwards. After 20
seconds, the cards
are turned face
downwards. A player
now seeks to identify
the card of the
opponent. If the guess
is correct, then that
player gets the card. If
the identification is
wrong, the card stays
face downwards. The
owner of the card can
look at it to check if
the guess is right.*

*The game continues
until either player has
five more cards
than the opponent.*

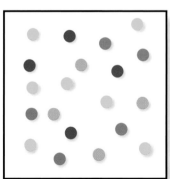

HERE ARE FOUR squares, each containing a number of dots. Which do
you judge to have the most dots? Put the squares in descending order,
from the most dots to the least. Check your answers on pages 70-71 ☞

FRAME OF JUDGEMENT

One player writes down a possible frame of judgement. Some examples are: "Would make a good birthday present"; "Useful in the kitchen"; "Dangerous if you are not careful"; "Needs skill to use".

This piece of paper is then placed face downwards on the table. The opponent now turns over the cards one by one. The first player has to judge instantly whether ▸

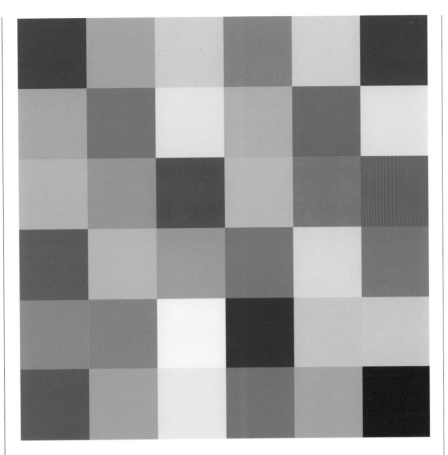

THE ABOVE PICTURE shows a selection of different colours. Which of the colours above exactly match the six used below?

Check your answers on pages 70-71 ☞

▸ the turned-up card fits the frame of judgement. So two piles grow: the accepted items and the rejected items. The person making the judgements wins if the number of cards in the acceptance pile is greater than 15. Otherwise, the opponent wins.

After the game is over, the opponent can challenge a particular judgement by reading the judgement frame from the piece of paper and pointing out that one or more cards do not match this frame. This is to prevent a player from cheating in order to reach the required number of cards.

The most important aspect of judgement is to *know what you are seeking to match*. It is one thing to match something against a formal definition or rule, but it is another thing to match something against the needs of the moment. Those needs can form a complex frame of judgement. For instance, a diner might judge a restaurant menu with the following frame in mind: "I want something that is meat not fish, and that does not have a heavy sauce with it." A choice is made according to whether an item on the menu matches that frame of judgement. If not, a compromise has to be made.

4 + 4 = 8

1.   2.   3.

A   2   3   4

5
2
1

A.   B.   C.

WHAT OTHER WAYS ARE THERE?

alternatives
alternatives

You may wish to have dinner at an Italian restaurant, or alternatively, at a Japanese restaurant. You get to the restaurant and look at the menu. The menu lists alternative dishes that you can choose.

A baby is expected. Sometimes, the parents know exactly the name that thay are going to give to their new son or daughter. It may be a traditional family name.

At other times, the parents discuss several alternative names. They may purchase a book that lists hundreds of alternative names. They can then gradually eliminate alternatives, until, finally, they have a shortlist of four or fewer names from which to choose.

Shuffle the pack of cards. Take the top four cards and lay them face upwards on the table in the sequence in which they were turned up.

Now construct a story around that sequence so that each item on the cards comes into the story in the right order. Next, try to construct another story for the same sequence of cards. Now change the sequence around, as you wish, and construct a third story. Change the sequence again and find a new story.

You can play this game on your own or with someone else. It is up to you to be satisfied with your own story.

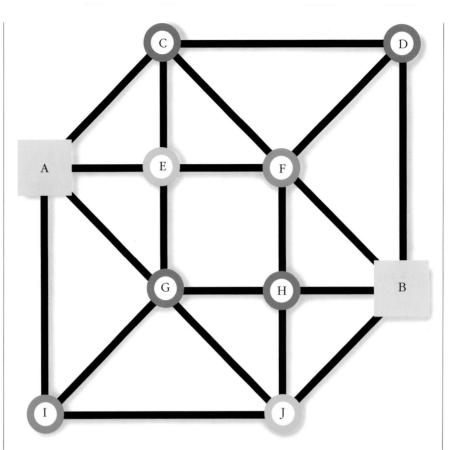

THE PICTURE SHOWS a type of maze. You start at point "A" and finish at point "B". What are the alternative routes if you must visit exactly four other points on the way? You cannot visit the same point more than once. Check your answers on pages 70-71 ☞

At a roundabout, the sign lists several ALTERNATIVE ROADS that you can take. You quickly try to figure out *which alternative would serve your purpose.*

Alternatives must serve the same purpose. A rose is not an alternative to a pair of shoes. We might, however, imagine a circumstance in which both a rose and a pair of shoes are being considered as alternative gifts. In this case, they would both serve the purpose of "giving a present".

To make the "Alternative Stories" game more difficult, you could deal out more cards. Or add a card into the middle of a story and adapt the story accordingly.

Sometimes, alternatives are presented to you, but at other times you have to create alternatives for yourself. If the alternatives are presented, then all you have to do is choose between them. This would be the case when you are choosing from a menu in a restaurant. In other cases, you have to create possible alternatives first and then choose from them. This would be the case if you were cooking for yourself.

FOUR TILES containing numbers and either an addition or subtraction sign are shown below. Write down five different ways in which you could reach the total of "22". You can try this using each number as often as you like. For instance, you could use "+4" six times and then use "-2" once.

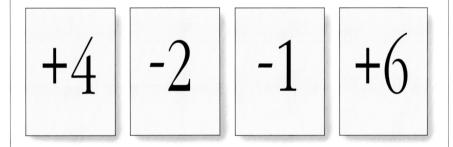

In many of the situations presented in this chapter, it is easy to check whether the alternative is a valid alternative. In the above exercise, for instance, you can test directly whether the proposed alternative fits the conditions that have been given. Four plus four equals eight. Five plus two plus one equals eight. But six plus three does not equal eight.

In other cases, however, the answer is not so easy. It may be a matter of individual judgement as to whether what is proposed is really an alternative. If you are thirsty and I offer you water or orange juice, those might be alternatives. But if I offer beer, that might be an alternative for some people, but not an alternative for others who do not drink beer.

THINKARD
GAME
**LOGICAL
SEQUENCE**

———

Shuffle the pack and then deal out five cards face upwards. Arrange these five cards in some sort of logical sequence. This should not be a story.

———

There must be some logical connection between one card and the next one. It is enough that there is a logical connection between the first card and the second card and that there is a different logical connection between the second card and the third card. In how many alternative ways can you arrange the sequence?

NUMBER
CARD GAME
**NUMBER
SEQUENCE
ALTERNATIVES**

---

*Shuffle the pack
and place it face
downwards. Turn
over the cards one by
one until two numbers
in a sequence are
turned up, one after
the other. Place these
cards side by side
to form the base
of the sequence.*

---

*Continue to turn over
the cards. A new card
may increase the
sequence upwards or
downwards. For
example, if the
established sequence
is 7 - 8, then either
6 or 9 can be added
to the sequence.
Cards that do not fit* ▶

In some situations, there are two levels of alternatives. The first level involves a search through our minds to find a possible logical connection between two situations or items. This means creating and considering alternatives. The second level is the search for different logical connections.

Usually, we look for alternatives only until we have found one that satisfies our needs of the moment. This is not good thinking. We need to look for other possible alternatives even when we already have one that works. There is no reason at all to believe that the first satisfactory alternative that we find is the best possible one.

We should always try to find BETTER ALTERNATIVES, even when we are already considering something that works quite well. *Finding better alternatives is how improvement and progress come about.*

THE PICTURE shows one method of attaching two pieces of wood to one another: joinery. Which alternative methods can you think of that would accomplish the same task? Check for possible answers on pages 70-71 ☞

▶ *the sequence are
discarded face
upwards on the table.*

---

*At any moment the
player can switch
from the first
established sequence to
a new sequence made
up from the discarded
cards on the table. But
the cards used in the
first sequence cannot
be re-used. Following
these conditions,
further sequences may
be started. The cards
in the old sequence
remain unusable.*

---

*The game ends when
all the cards in the
pack have been
turned over. The
objective is to build
old (or new)
sequences for as long
as possible without
having to discard a
card. To do this, the
player has to keep
an eye on emerging
alternative sequences
and then switch to
one of them.*

It is not an easy task to find all the possible alternatives that there are in a given situation. In some cases there may be so many alternatives to discover that the task would be impossible.

It is always worthwhile, however, to go beyond the obvious alternatives that are presented. This extra effort might well produce an original and valuable alternative that has not been included. This further work might reveal an alternative to you that is just as acceptable and valid in the situation.

THE PICTURES SHOW three different ways of finding out the height of a building: measuring one storey and multiplying that measurement as appropriate; dropping an object from the top of the building and timing its fall; lowering a string from the top of the building. What other ways can you think of? Which is the most efficient method? Which method would you choose? Pause and do your own thinking before reading on.

In the exercise featured above, the obvious alternatives are those that involve physically measuring the building with an appropriate measuring device, or alternatively, calculating the dimensions of the building by a mathematical method. You may consider measuring the shadow and working out the height of the building from that information if the circumstances allow. Or you could ask the architect.

comparison & choice

There are, of course, two aspects of comparison.

WHAT IS *different?*
WHAT IS THE SAME?

For many years scientists believed that an all-green and an all-red variety of an Australasian parrot were actually different species. Eventually, they discovered that the green and red birds were male and female of the Eclectus species.

COMPARISON enables us to *move forward to new things.*

FLOWERS that may seem very different can turn out to have so much in common that they belong to the same species. To which species do these two flowers belong? For the answer see pages 70–71 ☞

We come across something that is new. We look to see what there is about it that is "the same" as something we already know. This allows us to treat the new thing, cautiously, as we would have treated the thing we know. Then we start to focus on the differences between the new thing and the thing we know. Finally, we create a new "box" for the new thing and thereafter we can read it in terms of its own box (see page 17).

Science is based on using both these questions. For example, in the first analysis, a whale appears to be totally different from a human being. Yet, if we analyse the two in more depth, there are strong points of similarity. They both breathe air, they are both warm-blooded, they both give birth to live young – in fact, they are both mammals. Whales may also have an elaborate system of communication. Though sharks and dolphins look similar,

SPERM WHALE

BABY

dolphins are part of the whale family. Things that seem the same can be very different. Things that look different can be the same. New species are discovered this way. This is called "lumping" and "splitting". You lump together things which seem different, and split apart things that seem the same.

GREAT WHITE SHARK

Dinosaurs seem very different from birds, but there is good evidence to suggest that birds descended from dinosaurs. When there are existing

ROBIN

COMPSOGNATHUS

alternatives, or whenever we generate possible alternatives, we often compare them to see which one might be better. There may be two routes up a mountain. One is faster and more direct, but more dangerous. The other is slower, but easier and safer to climb. Which one you decide to choose will depend on your needs or personality.

Sometimes it is necessary to look hard in order to find small points of difference. In such cases, you set your mind to look for differences, and then you will find them. It does not mean that these differences are significant. People have different shaped ears. This point of difference has no practical value. An often used method for dismissing a new idea is to claim that the new idea is "the same as" the existing idea. In such cases, there is a need to "focus" on the difference between the new idea and the old one; it may seem small, but can lead in a whole new direction.

NUMBER CARD GAME
THE ADJACENT GAME

Deal out the cards, face upwards, in a line. Stop when any two adjacent cards add up to a total given by any other two adjacent cards. If there are two players or more, then the first player to spot the "similarity" is the winner. Take turns dealing.

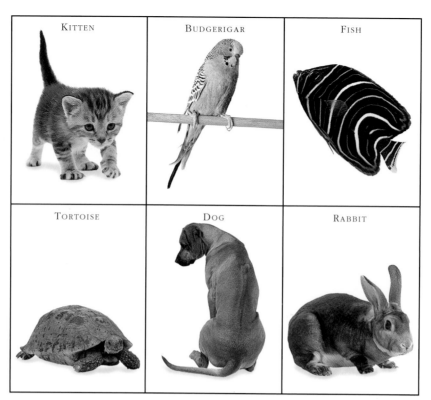

KITTEN · BUDGERIGAR · FISH

TORTOISE · DOG · RABBIT

IMAGINE YOU ARE considering keeping one of these animals as a pet. Compare them to one another as pairs. Focus on the points of difference.

CHOICE and DECISION are tied up with *alternatives, comparison,* and *judgement.* Without choice there are no alternatives, we judge which alternative is best.

COMPARE THREE DIFFERENT ways of getting to work: car, bus, and motor cycle. Consider points such as the following: you can read on a bus; you don't have to wait for a car or a motor cycle; a bus may be cheaper. Make a list of five negative points and five positive points about each mode of transport.

THINKARD GAME
THE FRAMEWORK GAME

Shuffle the pack and then turn over the top card in the pack. Look at this card and ask yourself the following question: "Under what conditions and in what frame of mind would I choose the item shown on this card?"

Repeat this process until you have chosen two further cards that might fit the same framework. Now that you have three possible alternatives, make a choice between the three.

MOTOR CYCLE

CAR

BUS

This is a game for two players. The pack is shuffled and three cards are dealt to each of the players who look at their cards but hide them from their opponent.

Each player in turn exposes the top card of the face-down pack. The player has to decide whether to keep that card or to discard it. Each player may hold only five cards in hand at any time. So when a player has five cards, he or she can only take a new card if an old ▶

Decision is a form of choice. The minimum choice is between doing something and not doing something: to buy a camera or not to buy a camera. There may be a third option: to postpone buying a camera. There may be a fourth option: to think further about buying a camera. The decision not to do something is still a decision, even though it often arises from the inability to make a decision.

There are always two aspects to any decision or choice.

the first aspect

is an exploration of the alternatives available. This may be an attempt to discover further alternatives. It may be possible to design a new alternative that combines two of the other alternatives. What would be the consequences of choosing a particular alternative? We would look at the immediate and longer-term consequences. We would look at the difficulties, problems, and potential dangers.

the second aspect

is to do entirely with the person who is making the particular choice or decision. What are the needs of that person? What are his or her tastes? What is the context of the choice? What are the priorities involved? What are the values? What is the objective that is trying to be reached in making the choice or decision?

▶ one is discarded. A player may turn over a fresh card from the pack and take this card, or may instead pick up the discarded card of the other player. The winner is the first player to obtain a sequence of four cards. If this proves too difficult, then a sequence of three cards is acceptable.

In this game, each player has to make an immediate decision: "Do I require this card or not?" This will depend on the cards the player already holds in his or her hand, and also on what he or she thinks the other player is collecting. There may also be another decision to be made: "Which card do I discard?"

WHAT ARE THE PARTS?

analysis

Analysis is one of the most fundamental processes of human thinking. How can you break down a complicated situation into smaller sections that you recognize? In every field, analysis is a key activity. Many things in the world are quite complicated. Most things that we know are quite simple. So we have to break down the complicated matters into the simple things that we know and can deal with more easily.

LOOK CLOSELY at this Islamic design, and you will see how a complex pattern can be created from surprisingly few simple shapes.

Success in thinking often depends on success in analysis. But there are two big dangers. Too many people are taught to believe that analysis and judgement are enough. They are not. Creativity and possibilities are the driving force of progress. The other danger is that the behaviour of a complex system cannot be detected in the behaviour of its parts. If you chop an animal into pieces, you no longer have a functioning animal.

THIS SQUARE has been made from the pieces shown beside it, without any overlapping. No piece has been used more than once. Not all the pieces have been used. Which pieces have been used to construct the shape? For the answer see pages 70-71 ☞

*One player looks
through the cards in
the pack and puts
together a collection
of four cards. There
must be some reason
for this collection.
The reason cannot
be a story told
around the cards.*

---

*The reason should be
written down on a
piece of paper. The
second player has to
seek to analyse the
reason behind the* ▶

Despite the dangers, analysis is a
VERY IMPORTANT PART of thinking.

LOOK CAREFULLY at these laid-out pieces of wood and decide
which item of furniture could be assembled from them.
Check your answer on pages 70-71 ☞

▶ *collection. This can
be done in two ways:
1. The player can
choose another card
and offer it. The
response could be: "It
fits"; "It might just fit";
"It definitely does
not fit".
2. The player can ask
a question that can be
answered by a simple
"yes" or "no".*

---

*Offering a card
counts as one point.
Asking a direct
question counts as
three points. Only
15 points can be
accumulated. Guesses
count as a question
except that a final
guess can be made
after the 15 points
have all been used up.
The two players then
reverse their roles.*

Sometimes the parts are separate and have been brought
together to form a whole. For example, a carpenter cuts the
lengths of wood that he or she wants and then assembles
them into a piece of furniture.

At other times, the parts are not separate but overlapping. It
is still a matter of sorting out the different elements that have
gone into the final situation.

NUMBER
CARD GAME
**ANALYSING
ACHIEVEMENT**

The pack is shuffled and five cards are dealt out face upwards. Is there any way in which four of the cards can be arranged so as to provide the value of the remaining card?

You can use addition, subtraction, multiplication, or division, but you must deal in whole numbers only. You can only use the given cards. Whichever player first spots a way of achieving the objective wins.

If no-one can see such a way, then a new card is turned over and one of the existing cards is discarded. The game continues until one player finds a way of achieving the task.

In analysing complex situations, with many connected parts, there is often a need to think of things which are not physically present, but those which exist in our minds.

THIS PICTURE SHOWS traffic congestion in a city. Analyse the factors involved: the causes, potential solutions, the rights and wrongs of the situation. Pause and do your own thinking before reading further.

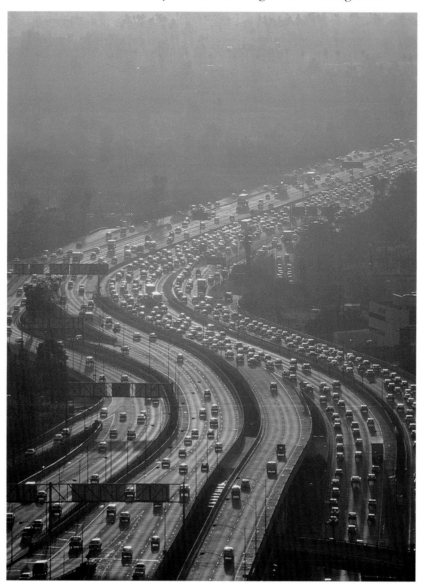

The factors you have analysed might include the following: the size of the roads; the need for travel and traffic; car ownership; the design and layout of the city; parking facilities; the enforcement of traffic regulations; the need to deliver goods in the city; and the behaviour of pedestrians.

IMAGE SOMEONE preparing a meal in a kitchen. Analyse the stages involved in preparing a meal. Pause and do your own thinking before reading further.

Your analysis might have included some of the following points – and some additional ones: deciding on the number of courses; deciding what each course will be; choosing which ingredients to use; deciding how much money to spend; getting the ingredients; preparing the ingredients; separating out the things which need to be cooked together; deciding what sequence to cook them in; putting things together; arranging presentation so that it looks good; keeping it warm; deciding what time to eat; deciding where to eat; making the seating arrangements; and finally, serving the meal.

There are times when an analysis *reveals the true parts* that are present or that have been assembled into the FINAL SITUATION. But there are other occasions when the parts are determined by *how we choose to look* at something. This is what we call PERCEPTION.

WHAT DO I SEE?

perception

Perception is by far *the most important part* of thinking. Perception is *the way we see the world* around us at any particular moment.

All perception is based on experience. Perception is based on our mood, our needs of the moment, and on our thinking skills.

When we see a plate of chicken and vegetables, our experience tells us what it is. Our experience reminds us how chicken and vegetables taste. But the way we see it also depends on ourselves. If we are hungry, we see it as attractive. If we have just eaten, then the chicken is much less attractive. If we know that there is a salmonella scare and that much chicken is infected, then we view the plate with suspicion. Our thinking skills direct our attention, and so affect our perception. We can direct our attention to the benefits and problems of eating that chicken. As a result we may make a decision.

THINKARD
GAME
**THE
PERCEPTION
GAME**

———

*This game is played by
two or more people.*

———

*Shuffle the pack. Turn
over one card and
place it face upwards.
Ten more cards are
dealt face upwards.*

———

*Each player chooses
from these cards one
that fits in with a
principle that he or
she has decided upon
based on the first card.
So one player forms a
group to the right of
the original card.* ▶

THE PICTURE SHOWS an outline shape. How would you describe this shape? Try to think of as many alternatives as you can. Pause and do your own thinking first before reading on.

▶ *The other player
forms a group to the
left. Each player must
have a basis for the
grouping. For
example, "things that
are used in the
garden". The basis
cannot be a story line.*

———

*Each player in turn
picks a card from the
cards lying face
upwards and adds it to
their group. Cards not
selected are put aside.
A new set of ten cards
is dealt face upwards.
The game ends when
there are no cards left
in the pack.*

———

*Without questioning,
each player has five
guesses to perceive the
basis for the group of
the other player. The
answer may be "yes",
"no", or, if the guess is
almost right, "close".*

You could see the picture as being made up of two overlapping squares. You could rest content with that or your thinking skills could urge you to look for more possibilities, more alternatives. Thinking on, you could see the picture as a three-dimensional drawing of two squares, one standing in front of the other. You could also see the shape as two "L"-shaped pieces. You may find yet further ways.

Which way of looking at something is the "RIGHT" one?

In some cases, there is a "right" answer when we are trying to recognize something. When you are driving along a road, and notice something strange on the road ahead, it is very important to get the answer "right". In many cases, however, perception is a matter of choice. Perception opens up possibilities. We can choose one of these or explore several possibilities.

THE PICTURE SHOWS a triangle of coins. The triangle is pointing upwards. How can you get the triangle to point downwards? Move the least number of coins you can in order to achieve this. Check your answers on pages 70-71 ☞

THINKARD GAME

CHANGE PERCEPTION GAME

The pack is shuffled and one card is drawn and placed face upwards on the table.

———

One player describes in simple terms the nature or function of the item on the card. The other player must describe the item in a different way. ▶

THIS PICTURE SHOWS some empty circles and some filled-in circles. How many filled-in circles does the picture show? Pause and think before reading further.

How did you reach your conclusion? Check your answers on pages 70-71 ☞

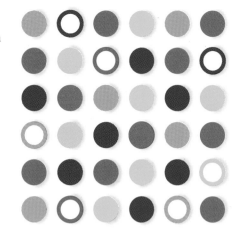

Check your answers on pages 70-71

▶ For example, if the item were a hose-pipe, one player might say: "a way of directing water to a specific place." The other player might say: "a way of avoiding wasting water where it is not wanted".

———

This can be a difficult game and it does not work equally well for all items. Sometimes the "changed" perception is not a true change but a different aspect. The important point is to try. If one card does not work well then move on to the next card.

Perception is concerned with change. How can we see the same thing in many different ways? You can look at a glass of fruit juice and say that it is half full. You can look at the same glass and say that it is half empty.

You see two people running, one after the other. In how many different ways could you look at this scene? Before reading on, write out a list of five possible interpretations. After reading on, try and add some more. There could be the following interpretations of the scene:

1. One person is trying to catch the other.

2. One person is trying to escape from the other.

3. They are both running away from something.

4. They are both running towards something or someone.

5. It has just started to rain and they are both running for shelter.

WHAT DOES THE PICTURE above depict? A fierce dog? Two cars heading towards each other and about to collide? How else could the dog and the cars be perceived?

COMMENT

You may think that the dog looks threatening, but it would be less so if you knew it was behind a fence.

NUMBER
CARD GAME
**NUMBER
CHOICE**

The pack of cards is shuffled and a card is dealt to each of the players in turn. If the value of the card is 12 or higher, then that card is placed face upwards in front of the player and no more cards are dealt to that player. This part of the game continues ▶

THE PICTURE ABOVE SHOWS a grid of painted squares. How many squares do you see?
Check your answers on pages 70-71 ☞

In many sitiuations, the change in our perception depends on what our minds choose to bring to the situation as possibilities. We might wish to broaden our perception. This is an important aspect of perception. How widely do we look? What other things do we take into account?

COMMENT

The two cars look as if they might collide, but equally they could be stationary or reversing.

▶ *until each player has a card valued at 12 or higher in front of him or her. All the remaining cards are collected up and re-shuffled.*

Each player now decides how the card in front of him or her can be broken down into a sum of three (only three) other numbers. For example 12 can be broken down into 6 + 4 + 2. For this game, there is no point in two of the numbers being the same.

Cards are now turned over one by one ▶

▶ *from the pack. Each* *player in turn is asked if he or she can "accept" that card. A player can only accept a card if one of three cases occurs:*

1. The card is exactly equal to one of any of the player's broken-up numbers (for example, 6 or 4 or 2 in the case of 12).

2. The card is equal to a combination of any of the broken-up numbers (for example, 6 + 2 or 2 + 4 in the case of 12).

3. The card is equal to any combination of ▶

THIS DETAIL FROM A PAINTING contains items of many different colours. Close your eyes and tell yourself you are going to look at red items. Now look at the picture. Repeat the exercise with yellow items, white items, and then with blue items. Each time you do this you will see the painting in a totally new way.

One very important aspect of perception is SELECTION. *What are the things that we choose to look at? Where do we DIRECT our attention?*

Sometimes, there are things that immediately catch our attention. At other times, our attention flows on from one thing to another. There are times when we need some framework for directing attention deliberately. This is what the CoRT Programme (see page 72), for the direct teaching of thinking in schools is all about.

▶ *the broken-up* *numbers added to the original number (for example, 12 + 2 or 12 + 6 + 4 in the case of 12).*

A player does not have to declare the broken-up numbers that he or she decides upon; however, the player may be challenged about his or her choice at the end of the game.

The game ends when there are no more cards left in the pack. The player with the most cards wins the game.

values
& feelings

In the end, values and feelings are the *most important* things *to anyone* who is doing any THINKING.

Values and feelings determine our objectives. Is this worth achieving? Why is this worth achieving? Values and feelings strongly affect our judgement of people, of things, and of courses of action. Values and feelings determine whether we are satisfied with the outcome of our thinking.

Does this mean that we should not bother to think but just depend on our feelings? Not at all.

The purpose of thinking is to arrange the world in our minds, so that we can APPLY our feelings EFFECTIVELY – not only for ourselves but *for other people, too.*

Feelings may tell you to fight someone with whom you disagree. Thinking may design an outcome that is satisfactory to both sides. There is nothing more dangerous than to assume that values and feelings without thinking are enough. Many of the world's wars and persecutions have arisen in this way.

THINKARD GAME
QUICK VALUES

The object of this game is to choose five cards that have the highest value for you. The game is best played with two players. One player turns over the cards rapidly from the face-down pack.

Each card of the pack is shown to the second player, who is allowed about three seconds to view each card and to decide whether to select it as one of his or her "valuable" five.

The player is not allowed to change his or her mind or go back to choose a card that has passed. All values are allowed except financial values. At the end of the game, the player must explain the value of each choice to the other player.

THINKARD GAME
CONSTRUCTIVE VALUES

In this game, the values have to fit together to achieve some purpose. Six cards are dealt to a player. These cards are exposed face upwards.

The player has to show how four of these cards can be used together to set up a business. This can be a business that makes money or it can be an operation that provides value to the community.

Players work co-operatively in this game, each offering suggestions. Once again, the value of selling one of the items on the cards to raise money or to make money is not permitted, because it would make the game much too easy.

Without thought, feelings and values are dangerous. There are three important things that we need to consider:

the first thing

is to acknowledge and to be aware of what our values and feelings are in a situation.

the second thing

is to see how those values and feelings affect our thinking with regard to the situation.

the third thing

is to consider whether the values and feelings are justified or helpful in a particular situation.

NUMBER CARD GAME
EARLY CHOICE

This is a two-person game. The pack is shuffled and placed face downwards. Each player is then dealt one card, which is exposed. Each player in turn exposes a card from the pack. The player may keep this card or reject it. For each player, the first two cards accepted are placed alongside the first card to form a group of three cards. The sum total of the three cards is noted.

The objective of each player is to form as many groups as possible with a value that is the same as this first group or near to it. Players must now use the card that they expose. There are no more discards. A card may either be added to an existing group or may form ▶

There are at least two big problems with values and feelings. The first problem is that your values and feelings may not agree with the values and feelings of other people. They may not agree with those of society in general or those of a particular group. For example, environmentalists may have very different values and feelings from industrialists.

LOOK AT THE SIX different chairs pictured below. What do you feel about each of them? Note your feelings before reading on.

A   B   C

D   E   F

Now put yourself in the position of someone opening a new restaurant. Look at each chair again and note your feelings under these new circumstances. What are the values now involved? You might consider cost, convenience, ease of cleaning, robustness, and contribution to atmosphere.

The second problem with values and feelings is that something that has a high value at the moment might have a negative value later. The next drink at a party seems very attractive. But if you have a motor accident later or are stopped for drink driving, then there are a lot of negative values.

▶ the start of a new group. Once placed in a position on the table, a card may not then be shifted to a new group. When the pack is exhausted, all the cards that are not in a completed group are collected and shuffled again to form a new pack. The game continues until the new pack is also exhausted.

The scoring is as follows:
• Completed groups score 20 points.
• If a new group does not match the total of the first group, then the difference is subtracted from 20 to give a score for that group.
• Single cards are always counted as a minus score according to their face value.

This score is subtracted from the total score. The player with the highest score at the end is the winner. The point of the game is that the player has to choose right at the beginning the most useful "value" for the first group.

LOOK AT THE FOUR quarters of this face; what is your first impression? Now try to recognize the different feelings that are being expressed.
Check your answers on pages 70-71 ☞

Check your answers on pages 70-71 ☞

It can also work the other way around. It might be a bore and a nuisance for a child to clean his or her teeth, but later there can be benefits. It is hard to study for exams when all your friends are out having a good time. But later, when you are qualified, you may be doing much better than them.

Being sensitive to the feelings of others is part of the importance of feelings. To do that, we need to recognize the feelings of others. Some people are better at it than others.

There are, of course, negative values and positive values. These may differ from person to person and may also depend on the circumstances.

THINKARD
GAME
**DIFFERENT
VALUES**

___

*The pack is shuffled
and the top card is
given to one player.
The card is placed face
upwards on the table.*

___

*The player has
to suggest:
1. For whom and in
what circumstances
the item on the card
would provide
positive values.
2. For whom and in
what circumstances
the item on the card
would provide
negative values.*

___

*It is never permitted to
say that the item
could be sold to
provide positive values.
This also applies to
renting out the item.
This game is best
played co-operatively,
with all players
making suggestions.
The game continues
with a new card.*

HOW DO I DESIGN THIS?

design

is a matter of *putting things together* to ACHIEVE some OBJECTIVE.

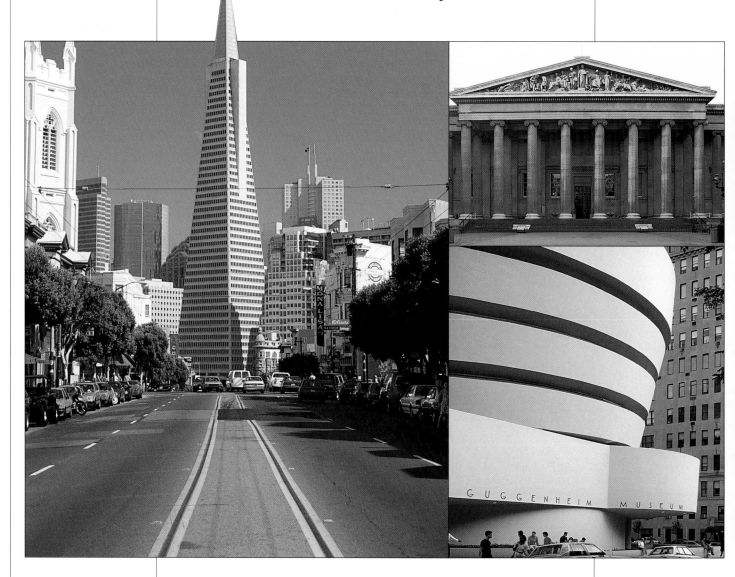

The pictures show different buildings from around the world. The ingredients for the buildings are very similar. What makes the difference is the design.

THINKARD
GAME
**DESIGN
A STORY**

The pack is shuffled and four cards are dealt face upwards to a player. The player may discard one of the cards and then start a story using the

Usually, there are a number of things that have to be kept in mind. In the case of a building, it must be good for its purpose (offices, residence, hospital, theatre), it must look good and fit into the surroundings, it must comply with building and fire regulations, and it must be done within the available budget.

You can, of course, use a standard design or copy someone else's design, but design usually involves some element of creativity. A designer tries to do something new and original. You can design a new train. You can design a shoe. You can design a flag for a new country. You can design a pipe.

THINKARD
GAME
**DESIGN
A GAME**

The task is to design a new game using the Thinkards. The game should be a collection type of game for two people. Each person is trying to collect

PIPE

TRAIN

SHOE

remaining three cards. The story may contain any number of characters. When the story has been set up, two more cards are dealt face upwards to the player who must continue the story using either one of the cards. The other card can be discarded. The game continues either until the player cannot continue or until six cards have been used in the story.

There are three things to be kept

in mind with any design:

1. What are you trying to ACHIEVE?

This is the *"objective"*.

2. What are the FACTORS or

CONSTRAINTS that you have to fit?

3. What MATERIALS or

INGREDIENTS are available?

something. What could that something be? How do the players get the cards? How can disputes be avoided? Be sure that the game can actually be played with the available Thinkards.

THINKARD
GAME

DESIGN A TOURIST ATTRACTION

Tourism, taken all together, is the biggest industry in the world. Tourism may involve travelling within your own country or going to another country.

You may travel because of the weather, in order to see some things, or to take part in some sport or activity. The task is to design a ▶

THE PICTURES SHOW different designs of sails that have been used from time to time in different countries. All the sails are designed to make use of natural wind power.

The materials are not identical but are similar.
What sort of things would have influenced the design of these sails?

Pause, and do your own thinking before reading further.

In most cases, the design of something evolves over a long period of time, with a series of small changes, rather than as a complete new design. In the above exercise, you might have considered the following factors: speed; manoeuvrability; sailing with or against the wind; ease of control; stability of the boat; the need to alter speed; long distance or in-shore use; cost.

▶ tourist attraction. This should be a new type of tourist attraction rather than a traditional one.

A player is dealt five cards face upwards. He or she must design a tourist attraction based on items in these five cards. If the player does not like these cards, then they are put aside and five new cards are dealt. If the player does not like these, then a final five cards are dealt. No more cards can be used. A design that uses all five cards is better than a design that only uses three. A design based on one card is not acceptable.

Design is much broader than just the VISUAL APPEARANCE of something.

So how do we judge which is the BEST?

NUMBER CARD GAME
DESIGN A CROSS

Using any of the number cards, how many simple crosses can you design? A cross consists of three cards in a column. The middle card is also the middle card of a row of three cards. So the cross consists of a central card with one card above and one below. Then there is one card to the right and another card to the left.

The object of the game is to make the sum of the three vertical cards exactly the same as the sum of the three horizontal cards. For example, the vertical column might be 4 - 6 - 1 and the horizontal row might be 3 - 6 - 2. Both column and row add up to the number 11.

THINKARD GAME
FUNCTIONS

Look through the Thinkards. See if you can find an item whose function could be carried out (perhaps not so well) by a combination of other cards. Two players looking through the cards can compete to see who finds the most examples.

THE PICTURES show three different bridges. Study each one carefully. Which one do you think is the better design?

By looking at the design, it is impossible to tell which is better. It would be necessary to know the span, the height of the banks, the amount of traffic going under and over the bridge, the cost, and numerous other factors.

problem solving

A problem is usually some difficulty or thing that we want to overcome or be rid of. The term "problem" can also be used when we are trying to achieve some task, though in many cases "design" or "task achieving" are more appropriate.

EACH OF THESE shapes can be divided into two equal halves so that each half could be fitted exactly over the other half. How could this be done? Check your answers on pages 70-71 ☞

When the course of action towards a desired objective is not easy or routine, then we say that we have a "problem".

The traditional method for problem solving is to find the cause of the problem and then to seek to remove that cause. If you feel a sharp pain when you sit upon a particular chair, you would seek out the cause and then remove it. Finding

NUMBER CARD GAME
EXACT NUMBER

Using only addition or subtraction, you have to achieve the exact number of 25. The players keep their cards concealed. At the beginning of the game, three cards are dealt to each player.

After that, the cards are turned up two at a time. If both players want the same card, they have to "buy" it by discarding some of the cards they hold. The player who offers to discard the most cards gets the desired card.

If both bids are equal, then no-one gets the card, but the discards still have to be made. In all other cases, only the winner who gets the card needs to make the discard. The first player to reach 25 wins.

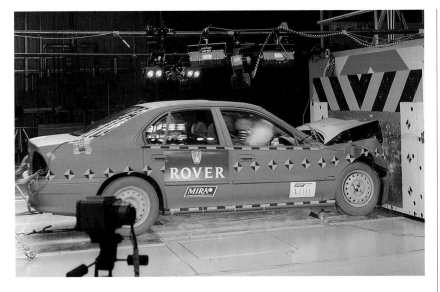

the cause may involve imagining some possible causes and then checking them out, one by one. If your television stops working, you could ask yourself: "Is the problem in the television?"; "Has the fuse in the plug blown?"; "Is there a problem at the broadcasting station rather than with your television?" With all problems we run through a list of possibilities before making a decision.

When traffic accidents occur, we try to find out what the causes may have been: weather conditions, loss of control, drink driving, brake failure, or falling asleep at the wheel.

We then try to solve these problems by introducing laws against speeding, by improving road signs, by inspecting vehicles more thoroughly, and by public awareness campaigns warning us of the dangers of drink driving.

THINKARD GAME
PROBLEM SOLVER

A person has fallen into the river and is being carried downstream. You want to rescue that person. You are dealt five cards from the pack. See whether any of these cards (or combinations) could somehow be used to solve the problem.

This game can be played co-operatively, with suggestions from the different players. Repeat the game with a new problem. There is a fire in the trees surrounding a house. How might any of the cards dealt be of use in solving this problem? A fresh set of cards should be dealt for each new problem. Repeat the game with a new problem.

*The pack is shuffled
and a card is turned
up. Each player has to
list on a piece of paper
all the potential
problems that can
arise in connection
with the item featured
on the card.*

*These might be
problems that occur in
the use of the item.
They might be
problems caused to
others or to the
environment by the
use of the item. There
might also be
problems caused by
over-use of the item.
For example, if the
item on the card is a* ▶

Sometimes, there is no *simple*
"SOLUTION" to the PROBLEM.

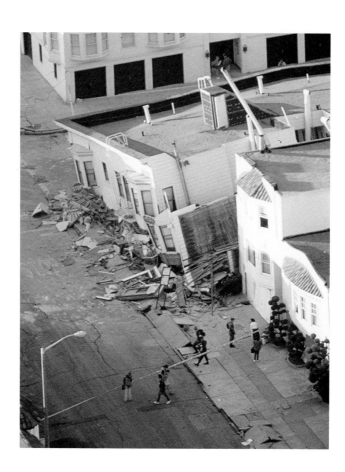

In such cases, the cause cannot be eliminated, and other strategies must be adopted. We have alarms and protection against burglary because we cannot remove the cause. We have buildings that are designed to resist earthquakes because we cannot prevent earthquakes from happening.

When we CANNOT SOLVE a problem

by removing the cause, then we have to

DESIGN A WAY FORWARD – even if the

CAUSE stays in place. We either act to

prevent or we *respond.*

▶ *hose-pipe, potential
problems in its use
include leakage and
difficulty in fitting it
to a tap. Problems
caused by use
include the excess
consumption of water,
both in the garden
and washing the car.*

*This puts demands on
water supplies and
this in turn can lead
to ecological problems.
In some areas, over-
irrigation can cause
salination of the soil.
When no player can
think of any more
problems, the lists are
compared, and the
winner is the player
with most problems
on the list.*

*If the players are not
familiar with the item
on the card, then
another card is
turned over.
The game continues
with new cards until
an agreed time.*

**PROBLEM
SOLVING
FUNCTION**

*Many of the items on
the Thinkards can be
seen as "solving" some
problem. For example,
an umbrella solves the
problem of getting wet
in the rain. A hose-
pipe solves the
problem of getting
water to where it is
needed without
having to carry it.*

*Sometimes, the item
allows us to do
something that we
could not do at all
before. At other times,
the item makes it
simpler or more ▶*

Every year throughout the world, people in developed countries produce an enormous amount of garbage. This is a problem that needs to be tackled in both these ways. We need to try to reduce the amount of garbage that is being and will be produced, but we also need to find ways of dealing with the garbage that has already been generated.

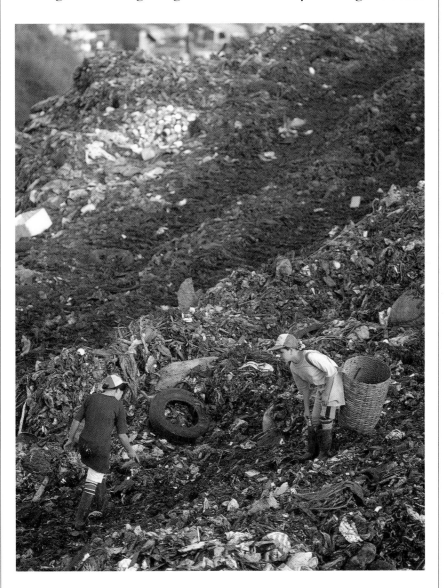

One of the key solutions to the garbage problem is re-cycling. Paper, glass bottles, and aluminium cans can all be re-cycled. Vegetable matter can be used as compost. Packaging material can be designed to be biodegradable. Perhaps packaging could have secondary uses. Are there any other ways to solve the problem of garbage?

*▶ convenient to do
something that we
could do before. So
many of the items
could be seen as
"solutions" to
a problem.*

*In this game, the
players work
co-operatively. The top
card of the pack is
turned over. The
players seek to
identify the problem
that the card solves
and to describe this
problem. They could
then go on to say
how this same
problem might be
tackled in a different
way. If a particular
card carries an item
that does not seem
to solve any problem,
the players move on
to the next card. In
any case, the next
card is turned over
when the first card
has been tackled.*

WHICH HAT SHALL WE WEAR?

the six
thinking hats

In cultures with a tradition of ARGUMENT, one person *takes a position* on a subject and another person *attacks that position*.

So "A" attacks "B" and "B" attacks "A". This method is used in law courts, in parliaments, in business negotiations, and in family discussions. In some cases, it is quite useful, but it is not the only way to explore a subject. Some cultures find the method too aggressive. It can also seem that each side is more interested in winning the argument than in actually exploring the subject.

A hat is a piece of clothing that you put on and take off quite easily. In many cultures, a hat is associated with the "role" that someone is playing at a particular moment. It is often associated with thinking: "Put on your thinking hat"; "Let's put on our thinking caps".

COMMENT

To play the *Six Hats Game* please refer to pages 3-4 of the *Mind Games* leaflet.

When we are thinking about something, we are usually trying to do everything at once. We might be looking out for dangers and difficulties – why something will not work. We might be trying to find new ideas. We might be looking for more information. Then there are our feelings and emotions that try to interfere all the time. Can we separate out all these difficult types of thinking?

A golfer has many different clubs in his or her bag. One club is suitable for some situations; other situations require a different club. You could play golf using only one club. But you would be beaten by a player who used a full set.

Why do we ASSUME that there is ONE SETTING that will be adequate for all our thinking? *Why* do we try to do EVERYTHING AT ONCE?

The Six Thinking Hats method is now in use worldwide in all manner of organizations, ranging from major businesses to families and schools. It is used because it is simple and practical. When an issue is discussed, everyone present applies a particular hat to that issue and thinks in the same direction.

The six hats of different colours represent EVERY BASIC TYPE OF THINKING.

the white hat

White suggests paper. The white hat concerns information. When we wear the white hat, we ask the following kinds of questions: "What information do we have?"; "What information do we need?"; "What information is missing?"; "How are we going to get the information we need?"; "What questions should we be asking?" The white hat is used to direct attention to available or missing information.

the red hat

Red suggests fire and warmth. The red hat is to do with feelings, intuition, and emotions. You may not know the reasons why you like something, or why you do not like something. When the red hat is in use, you have the opportunity to put forward your feelings and intuitions without any explanation at all. Your feelings exist, and the red hat gives you permission to put these feelings forward.

the black hat

This is probably the most useful hat. It is certainly the hat that is most often used. Black reminds us of a judge's robes. The black hat is for caution. The black hat stops us from doing things that may be harmful. The black hat points out the risks, and why something may not work. Without the black hat we would be in trouble all the time. However, the black hat should not be over-used, as over-use may be dangerous.

the green hat

Green suggests vegetation, which suggests growth, energy, and life. The green hat is the energy hat. Under the green hat, you put forward proposals and suggestions and propose new ideas and alternatives. Under the green hat, you suggest modifications and variations for a suggested idea. The green hat allows you to put forward possibilities. When the green hat is in use, everyone makes an effort to be creative.

the blue hat

The blue hat is for looking at the thinking process itself: "What should we do next?"; "What have we achieved so far?" We use the blue hat at the beginning of a discussion in order to define what we are thinking about, and to decide what we want to have achieved at the end of our thinking. The blue hat may be used to order the sequence of hats that we are going to be using, and to summarize what we have achieved.

the yellow hat

Yellow suggests sunshine and optimism. Under the yellow hat we make a direct effort to find the values and benefits in a suggestion: "What is good about this?" Even if we do not like the idea, the yellow hat asks us to seek out the good points. "Where are the benefits?"; "Who is going to benefit?"; "How will the benefits come about?"; "What are the different values?"

CONCLUSION
start again

At this point, you may have enjoyed parts of the book. Some of it will perhaps be a bit confusing. With time, things will become clearer and simpler as your thinking skills get better and better. Treat the book as a tennis court. Practise the different strokes on your own, or with a partner.

In time, you will know how to think. You will know how to watch yourself thinking. You will know how to watch others thinking. You will be in control of your own thinking. With repetition, the games will help you develop thinking as a skill.

At first, activities such as riding a bicycle and driving a car are difficult, and not very enjoyable. But as your skill grows, so does your enjoyment, and your sense of "being in control". It is the same with thinking.

Once you have started to

enjoy thinking – KEEP GOING.

Start the book again and again.

Thinking need not be boring. Thinking need not be frightening. Thinking need not be intimidating. Thinking can be your hobby. The most important thing you can take from the book is that thinking is enjoyable.

answers

pp. 12–17 Recognition

p. 14 Of the four types of mushrooms, *A* and *C* are edible. *B* is *Amanita muscaria* (fly agaric), a poisonous mushroom whose toxins attack the central nervous system, producing effects such as hallucination, euphoria, hyperactivity, coma, and possible death. *D* is *Amantia phalloides* (death cap), a deadly poisonous mushroom which, even in very small amounts, causes diarrhoea and vomiting, and although the victim appears to recover, the poison is still circulating in the bloodstream and causes fatal liver and kidney failure.

A B C

p. 15 The three objects shown in silhouettes are: *A* coffee pot; *B* jug; *C* plate and knife.

p. 15 Familiar faces: *A* Madonna; *B* Princess Diana; *C* Arnold Schwarzenegger; *D* Nelson Mandela. The face on the jigsaw puzzle is Albert Einstein.

A B C D

p. 16 The painting is *The Circus* (1890–91) by the Pointillist painter, Georges-Pierre Seurat (1859–91).

p. 17 The flags represent: *A* Australia *B* Norway; *C* Belize; *D* Ireland; *E* Liberia; *F* India; *G* Iceland; *H* New Zealand.

pp. 18–21 Concepts

p. 18 Three possible pairing arrangements are: car and typewriter (mechanical extension devices); pencil and snake (long and thin); horse and hen (farm animals).

p. 21 There are two differences between the hot air balloon and the zeppelin. The zeppelin uses a gas that is always lighter than air (helium or hydrogen), while the hot air balloon heats up ordinary air. Secondly, the hot air balloon just follows air currents, while the zeppelin has engines to enable it to chart a course.

The plane and helicopter are different in the ways they achieve flight. The entire body of the plane must travel through the air to achieve lift, whereas it is only the rotor blades of the helicopter that must move. This difference means that the helicopter can move directly upwards, downwards, and forwards; a plane can only move forwards.

The rocket is different from all of them because it does not "fly" through the air. The energy of the burning fuel lifts it off the ground, and momentum keeps it going when the fuel is gone.

A B C

pp. 22–25 Possibilities

p. 22 The distorted objects are: *A* fir cone; *B* tuba; *C* rose.

p. 23 The odd shape out is *C* because it is the only shape that is not equilateral.

p. 24 Balancing the box on its edge is achieved by fixing a heavy weight by a vertical strip to the far side of the box. The weight hangs below the table and keeps the box upright on its edge.

p. 25 In the maze puzzle, the rule for the black route is as follows: if you meet a red square on your right, turn right after passing it and keep going straight until you come to the next red square; if you meet a red square on your left, turn left after passing the red square and keep going until you come to the next red square. The rule for the red route is as follows: if you meet a blue followed by a yellow on either side, turn right after passing them; if you meet a yellow followed by a blue on either side, turn left after passing them. Otherwise keep straight on.

pp. 26–29 Judgement

p. 27 The lines that are equal in length to *A* are: *B*, *C*, *E*, *H*, *I*, and *L*.

p. 28 The four countries are: *A* Australia; *B* China; *C* USA; *D* Brazil.

p. 28 All four squares have exactly the same number of dots: 20.

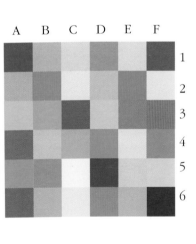

A B C D E F
1 2 3 4 5 6

D5 E1 A4 D4 D2 A1

p. 29 The matching tints are: D5, E1, A4, D4, D2, and A1.

pp. 30–35 Alternatives

p. 32 There are 28 routes through the maze from A to B: EGHJ; EGJH; ECDF; ECFD; ECFH; EFHJ; EFCD; EGHF; EGIJ; GEFH; GJHF; GIJH; GECD; GECF; GEFD; GHFD; CDFH; CEFH; CEGH; CEGJ; CEFD; CFHJ; IJHF; IGHF; IJGH; IGEF; IGHJ; IGJH.

p. 34 The alternative methods that can be used to attach one piece of wood to another include the following: nails; screws; binding; glue; staples; dowels; bolts and nuts; plates and brackets; rivets and washers.

pp. 36–41 Comparison & Choice

p. 38 Both of the flowers shown in the illustration are popular types of chrysanthemum.

pp. 42–45 Analysis

p. 42 The four pieces that have been used to form the square are: *A*, *C*, *E*, and *F*.

p. 43 The item of furniture that is made from the various pieces of wood is a chair.

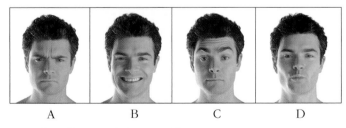

pp. 46–51 Perception

p. 48 The task is made very much easier if you look at the triangle of coins as a rosette with three extra coins attached. All you need to do is to move each coin round to the next position and the triangle now points downwards.

p. 49 You may have decided to count the filled-in circles. Or, you may see it as an arrangement of 6 x 6 = 36 circles. You count up the empty circles and subtract the total from 36.

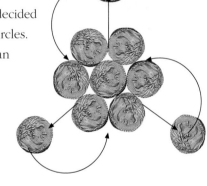

p. 50 There are 14 squares in the grid.

pp. 52–55 Values & Feelings

p. 55 The following are suggestions for the four expressions: *A* puzzled, concerned, tense, etc. *B* happy, relaxed, *C* quizzical, bemused; *D* seductive, thoughtful, contemplative.

A   B   C   D

pp. 60–63 Problem Solving

p. 60 The shapes can be divided in exact halves as shown.

acknowledgments

PICTURE ACKNOWLEDGMENTS
Key: t=top; b=bottom; c=centre; l=left; r=right; a=above

Dorling Kindersley would like to thank the following for their kind permission to reproduce the photographs:

Hulton-Deutsch Collection
p.11 bl, p.15 bc

Courtesy of IKEA Ltd.
p.54 ca, cra, cb, c, crb

Magnum Photos Ltd.
Philip J. Griffiths p.53 t

MIRA
p.61 t

Musée de Louvre, Paris
p.10 (detail), p.51 *The Marriage At Cana* by Veronese

Musée d'Orsay, Paris
p.11 (detail), p.16 *The Circus* by Seurat

National Motor Museum, Beaulieu
p.40 bl, bc

Panos Pictures
Marc Schlossman p.63 c

Retna Pictures Ltd.
Steve Granitz p.15 clb, p.70 cl; Michael Melia p.15 bl, p.70 cl; Clemens Rikken p.15 br, p.70 cl; Rocky Widner p.15 crb, p.70 cl

Rex Features Ltd.
Sipa Press p.62 t; p.64 c

Royal Horticultural Society
p.38 tl

Science Photo Library
Scott Camazine p.8 cr; Custom Medical Stock Photo p.7

Tony Stone Images
Ken Biggs p.44 c

Studio Editions Ltd.
p.20 c, p.64 clb, bl, tr, p.65 tl, p.71

SPECIAL PHOTOGRAPHY
Jane Burton p.40; Andy Crawford p.39 r; Neil Fletcher p.14 b; Steve Gorton p.40 cl; Frank Greenaway pp.38-39; Marc Henrie p.26 t; Dave King p.38 b, p.40 bl, bc, pp.40-41, p.55; Cyril Laubscher p. 37, p.39 l; Tracy Morgan pp.26-27, p.40 c; David Murray p.31 cl; David and Michael Murray p. 54 tl; Stephen Oliver p.56 cr; Tim Ridley pp.10 br-11 b; Matthew Ward p.59 c; Jerry Young p. 40 tr

ILLUSTRATIONS
Karen Cochrane p.20 crb (hovercraft), p.21 tl, tr (helicopter, rocket)
Vanessa Lough p.49 b
Mandy Pritty p.2, p.12, p.30, p.36, p.46, p.69
Mark Davies p.13, p.24, pp.34-35, p.48 br, p.70 br
Phil Ormerod p.23, p.25, p.28 b, pp.32-33, p.42, pp.48 t-49 t, p.60
Zirrinia Austin p.29

Dorling Kindersley would like to thank Paddy Hills, Dr. de Bono's assistant, whose helpfulness made this book possible; Dover Publications Inc, New York, for permission to include several Dover images in the book; Kirstie Hills for editorial assistance; Darren Hill for design assistance.

For more information about Dr. de Bono's
• Public seminars
• Private seminars
• Certified Training Programs
• Thinking programs for schools
• CD Rom
• Books and tapes
• CoRT Thinking Lessons

Please call or write to:
Diane McQuaig
The McQuaig Group
132 Rochester Ave.
Toronto, Ontario
Canada, M4N 1P1

Tel: (416) 488 0008 Fax: (416) 488 4544